No Feedback
Performance in Co

GW01217835

Feldman,
Maxwell,
Plants,
Sells.
(eds.)

FORM 1

nfc_books IIII

Published by nfc_books

nofeedback.org.uk

thought
provoking —
especially
the end of the
meeting.

Thought
provoking
absolutely
great show!
x.

SOMETIMES
WE NEED TO
Feel like
the odd one
out

Why do
do I do
anythi
Stop it

DIFFERENT!
UNIQUE
...
☺

I wanted to
get up and say
no but I was
scared.

Really thought-provoking,
I wanted it to go
further, more option
to respond to
the research
or science

Everyo
along
....
Right
th

Alie Ghodi
was
Buddhist?

~~Brilliant~~ it was a great
piece!
Could go
further → people
should feel more
uncomfortable

Give people
more space
to react

!

Interesting
piece
- really made
me think.
Can feel what
in fair group
feels.

Clever
— is this actually
always going to
be a play?
When will we really
obey something
real?

I can't believe
how easy it
is to be go
along with
everything that I
was told to do

I beha
like a
sh

Interesting +
unique...
Could go
further...
Deep

WORRYING HOW
QUICKLY I
SUCCUMBED TO
PSYCHOLOGICAL
EFFECTS I'M
AWARE OF
GOOD EVENING

PROUD TO
REBEL!

Fright

Enjoyed the
introduction into
world of the
wanted to
singer at the
like an

Brilliant!!...

GO TO
BIG THEATRES

Unfortu
so man
to toda
Lets

No Feedback has a permanent company and set of partners now, but we wouldn't have got to where we are without these people (this list is not exhaustive):

Ali Kaviani Alice Kentridge Alice Mackenzie Ana Martinez Andrea Balducci Andreas Philippopoulos-Mihalopoulos Annabel Rook Annie Jael Kwan Becky Evans Brennan Pardee Dámaso Randulfe Dan Ball Daniela Nadj Elisa de Grey Erik Perera Finger In The Pie Theatre Ltd Francisco Carballo Gill James Gregory Stanton Guido Tallman Guy Taylor Harrington Id Helen Czerski Holly Moy J Maxwell James Headly Jeremy Wells Jessica Brewster Jessica Moolenaar Joe Harris Joe Iredale Jon Cooper Joni Steiner Judith Foys Karin Vah Katherine Gill Lily Mari Linda Litchfield Lindsay Bremner Lizzy Fretwell Louise Mari Lucy Irvine Lucy Livingstone Marco Monterzino Mauro de Giorgi Meadhbh Boyd Nazha Harb Nyree Yergainharsian Patrick Young Ra Optimus Raffaella Baruzzo Raphael Planas Rebecca Benz Rebecca Clark Richard Preston Roland Smith Rosie Barratt Rosie Hunter Samir Pandya Stella Nikolakaki Stuart Heyes and all at Fuel Sue Davies Suko Yoshimi Thomas Needham Todd Plants University of Wisconsin-Madison, Department of English Viv Broughton Will Jennings

Contents

7 No Feedback: An Introduction   Lizzie Sells

8 The Ten Stages of Genocide   Gregory Stanton

14 Normality vs Atrocity: Can we   Debora Miná
be playful when talking about Genocide?

20 The Atmosphere of Genocide   Andrea Philappopoulos-Mihalopoulos

23 The Physicality of the   Irène Wernli
Pink Lady Puppets

26 Place and Space   Lizzie Sells

29 On Empathy   Jen Plants

34 Parched Anchovies   Marco Monterzino
and Feather Ticklers

36 Trials as Theatre: Daniela Nadj
A Case Study

42 Resisting Genocidal Forces   Shana Swiss

46 The Challenge of Creating   Carolin Ott
a Character for No Feedback

48 Wearing Manipulation   Debora Miná

51 The Scientist and the Social   Genevieve Maxwell
Construction of Scientific Fact

58 The Anatomy of No Feedback   Nina Feldman

65 Theatre Delicatessen   Jessica Brewster

66 Partners

70 The Company

No Feedback: An Introduction

Lizzie Sells

No Feedback is described as an interactive theatrical event highlighting discrimination and dehumanisation. What do we mean by that? Our aim is to interrogate the anthropological dimension of a social phenomenon that has recurrently happened throughout history. In the middle of the Twentieth Century when its horrors were becoming clearer and clearer, Raphael Lemkin named this phenomenon genocide. By combining the classical Greek word for people or clan (genos) with the Latin suffix for killing (cide), Lemkin wanted to convey a crime of historical proportions: the biological obliteration of national, racial or religious groups. Since 1945 we are fortunate enough to have the Convention on the Prevention and Punishment of the Crime of Genocide (CPPCG), unanimously approved by the United Nations General Assembly in 1948. Ever since, international law has the right framework to typify and persecute such a crime. However, the questions still stand: How can genocide possibly happen? How is a situation created in which hundreds or thousands or millions of people be condemned to death or be socially ostracised by virtue of their race, ethnicity, nationality, religion, language, political or cultural preferences?

In dealing with this subject we need to be both realistic and humble. Genocide is not the sole patrimony of distant lands that every so often descend into unspeakable acts of barbarity, but a spectre that haunts every human community. In that sense, it is not enough to show our solidarity with the victims of genocide by maintaining their memory and keeping a thorough record of the crime. It is crucial to be aware of the inner workings of genocide. The insidious ways in which we are all capable of discriminating against each other. All of us are in perennial danger of being victims of this behaviour as well as perpetrators. Whether actively or complicity, at the end of the day, it doesn't matter.

This frightening latency of genocide is what *No Feedback* set off to explore. We do this by inviting the audience to participate in a piece of interactive theatre. We create a situation where active participation is the name of the game. Our task is to make the public (and us, the performers) face the facts: genocide can occur anywhere and to anyone once people start to be classified. Classification is more often than not an arbitrary exercise. We are interested in pondering how it is actually possible to differentiate between human beings. In order to investigate this process, we take the concept of differentiation to the extreme, until it reaches absurd levels. At the end of the day, we want to map out the ways in which a group of people is willing to "Play God" and decide over the life and death of others.

1. classification:

All cultures have categories to distinguish people into "us and them" by ethnicity, race, religion, or nationality: German and Jew, Hutu and Tutsi. Bipolar societies that lack mixed categories, such as Rwanda and Burundi, are the most likely to have genocide. The main preventive measure at this early stage is to develop universalistic institutions that transcend ethnic or racial divisions, that actively promote tolerance and understanding, and that promote classifications that transcend the divisions. The Catholic church could have played this role in Rwanda, had it not been riven by the same ethnic cleavages as Rwandan society. Promotion of a common language in countries like Tanzania has also promoted transcendent national identity. This search for common ground is vital to early prevention of genocide.

2. symbolization:

We give names or other symbols to the classifications. We name people "Jews" or "Gypsies", or distinguish them by colors or dress; and apply the symbols to members of groups. Classification and symbolization are universally human and do not necessarily result in genocide unless they lead to dehumanization. When combined with hatred, symbols may be forced upon unwilling members of pariah groups: the yellow star for Jews under Nazi rule, the blue scarf for people from the Eastern Zone in Khmer Rouge Cambodia. To combat symbolization, hate symbols can be legally forbidden (swastikas) as can hate speech. Group marking like gang clothing or tribal scarring can be outlawed, as well. The problem is that legal limitations will fail if unsupported by popular cultural enforcement. Though Hutu and Tutsi were forbidden words in Burundi until the 1980's, code words replaced them. If widely supported, however, denial of symbolization can be powerful, as it was in Bulgaria, where the government refused to supply enough yellow badges and at least eighty percent of Jews did not wear them, depriving the yellow star of its significance as a Nazi symbol for Jews.

3. discrimination:

A dominant group uses law, custom, and political power to deny the rights of other groups. The powerless group may not be accorded full civil rights, voting rights, or even citizenship. The dominant group is driven by an exclusionary ideology that would deprive less powerful groups of their rights. The ideology advocates monopolization or expansion of power by the dominant group. It legitimizes the victimization of weaker groups. Advocates of exclusionary ideologies are often charismatic, expressing resentments of their followers, attracting support from the masses. Examples include the Nuremberg Laws of 1935 in Nazi Germany, which stripped Jews of their German citizenship, and prohibited their employment by the government and by universities. Denial of citizenship to the Rohingya Muslim minority in Burma is a current example. Prevention against discrimination means full political empowerment and citizenship rights for all groups in a society. Discrimination on the basis of nationality, ethnicity, race or religion should be outlawed. Individuals should have the right to sue the state, corporations, and other individuals if their rights are violated.

4. dehumanization:

One group denies the humanity of the other group. Members of it are equated with animals, vermin, insects or diseases. Dehumanization overcomes the normal human revulsion against murder. At this stage, hate propaganda in print and on hate radios is used to vilify the victim group. The majority group is taught to to regard the other group as less than human, and even alien to their society. They are indoctrinated to believe that " We are better off without them." The powerless group can become so depersonalized that they are actually given numbers rather than names, as Jews were in the death camps. They are equated with lth, inpurity, and immorality. Hate speech lls the propaganda of of cial radio, newspapers, and speeches.

To combat dehumanization, incitement to genocide should not be confused with protected speech. Genocidal societies lack constitutional protection for countervailing speech, and should be treated differently than democracies. Local and international leaders should condemn the use of hate speech and make it culturally unacceptable. Leaders who incite genocide should be banned from international travel and have their foreign nances frozen. Hate radio stations should be jammed or shut down, and hate propaganda banned. Hate crimes and atrocities should be promptly punished.

5. organization:

Genocide is always organized, usually by the state, often using militias to provide deniability of state responsibility (the Janjaweed in Darfur.) Sometimes organization is informal (Hindu mobs led by local RSS militants) or decentralized (terrorist groups.) Special army units or militias are often trained and armed. Plans are made for genocidal killings. Acts of genocide are disguised as counter-insurgency if there is an ongoing-armed confict or civil war. The era of "total war" began in World War II. Firebombing did not differentiate civilians from non-combatants. The civil wars that broke out after the end of the Cold War have also not differentiated civilians and combatants. They cause widespread war crimes. Mass rapes of women have become a characteristic of all modern genocides. Arms flows to states and militias (often in violation of UN Arms Embargos) facilitate acts of genocide. States organize secret police to spy on, arrest, torture, and murder people suspected of opposition to political leaders. Motivations for targeting a group are indoctrinated through mass media and special training for murderous militias and special army killing units. To combat this stage, membership in these militias should be outlawed. Their leaders should be denied visas for foreign travel and their foreign assets frozen. The UN should impose arms embargoes on governments and citizens of countries involved in genocidal massacres, and create commissions to investigate violations, as was done in post-genocide Rwanda, and use national legal systems to prosecute those who violate such embargos.

6. polarization:

Extremists drive the groups apart. Hate groups broadcast polarizing propaganda. Laws may forbid intermarriage or social interaction. Extremist terrorism targets moderates, intimidating and silencing the center. Moderates from the perpetrators' own group are most able to stop genocide, so are the first to be arrested and killed. Leaders in targeted groups are the next to be arrested and murdered. The dominant group passes emergency laws or decrees that grants them total power over the targeted group. The laws erode fundamental civil rights and liberties. Targeted groups are disarmed to make them incapable of self-defense, and to ensure that the dominant group has total control. Prevention may mean security protection for moderate leaders or assistance to human rights groups. Assets of extremists may be seized, and visas for international travel denied to them. Coups d'état by extremists should be opposed by international sanctions. Vigorous objections should be raised to disarmament of opposition groups. If necessary they should be armed to defend themselves.

7. preparation:

National or perpetrator group leaders plan the "Final Solution" to the Jewish, Armenian, Tutsi or other targeted group "question." They often use euphemisms to cloak their intentions, such as referring to their goals as "ethnic cleansing," "puri cation," or "counter-terrorism." They build armies, buy weapons and train their troops and militias. They indoctrinate the populace with fear of the victim group. Leaders often claim that "if we don't kill them, they will kill us," disguising genocide as self-defense. There is a sudden increase in inflammatory rhetoric and hate propaganda with the objective of creating fear of the other group. Political processes such as peace accords that threaten the total dominance of the genocidal group or upcoming elections that may cost them their grip on total power may actually trigger genocide. Prevention of preparation may include arms embargos and commissions to enforce them. It should include prosecution of incitement and conspiracy to commit genocide, both crimes under Article 3 of the Genocide Convention.

8. persecution:

Victims are identi ed and separated out because of their ethnic or religious identity. Death lists are drawn up. In state sponsored genocide, members of victim groups may be forced to wear identifying symbols. Their property is often expropriated. Sometimes they are even segregated into ghettos, deported into concentration camps, or confined to a famine-struck region and starved. They are deliberately deprived of resources such as water or food in order to slowly destroy them. Programs are implemented to prevent procreation through forced sterilization or abortions. Children are forcibly taken from their parents.

The victim group's basic human rights become systematically abused through extrajudicial killings, torture and forced displacement. Genocidal massacres begin. They are acts of genocide because they intentionally destroy part of a group. The perpetrators watch for whether such massacres meet any international reaction. If not, they realize that the international community will again be bystanders and permit another genocide.

At this stage, a Genocide Emergency must be declared. If the political will of the great powers, regional alliances, or U.N. Security Council or the U.N. General Assembly can be mobilized, armed international intervention should be prepared, or heavy assistance provided to the victim group to prepare for its self-defense. Humanitarian assistance should be organized by the U.N. and private relief groups for the inevitable tide of refugees to come.

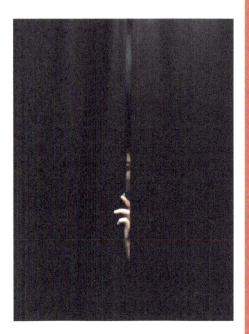

9. extermination:

Extermination begins, and quickly becomes the mass killing legally called "genocide." It is "extermination" to the killers because they do not believe their victims to be fully human. When it is sponsored by the state, the armed forces often work with militias to do the killing. Sometimes the genocide results in revenge killings by groups against each other, creating the downward whirlpool-like cycle of bilateral genocide (as in Burundi). Acts of genocide demonstrate how dehumanized the victims have become. Already dead bodies are dismembered; rape is used as a tool of war to genetically alter and eradicate the other group. Destruction of cultural and religious property is employed to annihilate the group's existence from history. All men of fighting age are murdered in some genocides. All women and girls are raped. In total genocides all the members of the targeted group are exterminated.

At this stage, only rapid and overwhelming armed intervention can stop genocide. Real safe areas or refugee escape corridors should be established with heavily armed international protection. (An unsafe "safe" area is worse than none at all.) The U.N. Standing High Readiness Brigade, EU Rapid Response Force, or regional forces — should be authorized to act by the U.N. Security Council if the genocide is small. For larger interventions, a multilateral force authorized by the U.N. should intervene. If the U.N. Security Council is paralyzed, regional alliances must act anyway under Chapter VIII of the U.N. Charter or the UN General Assembly should authorize action under the Uniting for Peace Resolution GARes. 330 (1950), which has been used 13 times for such armed intervention. Since 2005, the international responsibility to protect transcends the narrow interests of individual nation states. If strong nations will not provide troops to intervene directly, they should provide the airlift, equipment, and financial means necessary for regional states to intervene.

10. denial:

Denial is the final stage that lasts throughout and always follows genocide. It is among the surest indicators of further genocidal massacres. The perpetrators of genocide dig up the mass graves, burn the bodies, try to cover up the evidence and intimidate the witnesses. They deny that they committed any crimes, and often blame what happened on the victims. They block investigations of the crimes, and continue to govern until driven from power by force, when they flee into exile. There they remain with impunity, like Pol Pot or Idi Amin, unless they are captured and a tribunal is established to try them. The response to denial is punishment by an international tribunal or national courts. There the evidence can be heard, and the perpetrators punished. Tribunals like the Yugoslav, Rwanda or Sierra Leone Tribunals, the tribunal to try the Khmer Rouge in Cambodia, or the International Criminal Court may not deter the worst genocidal killers. But with the political will to arrest and prosecute them, some may be brought to justice.

Normality vs Atrocity:
Can we be playful when talking about Genocide?

Debora Miná

In November 2013 Nina, Marco and I met to develop the project in a Theatre Delicatessen room in Marylebone (long before we started our collaboration). It was months after the first scratch performance at Battersea Arts Centre. We didn't have much but anchovies and the 8 stages of Genocide, and we wanted to make a show.

We asked ourselves - how do we start? How do we embody this theme? And moreover, do we have any right to talk about something none of us has experienced?

I remember going through a lot of emotions that day. The excitement of working on a new project mixed with the discomfort of addressing such a subject. We would sit and discuss ideas and then I would find myself literally curling into a ball and feeling like I didn't want to talk about the stages of genocide any more. I was alternately engaging with and rejecting the work. I felt I was a fraud and that I didn't have any legitimacy to embark on this quest. The only way I could justify myself was to remember that we were speaking from our own points of view, as bystanders, as people who had read stories of genocide in books and maybe listened to survivors of the holocaust giving a talk, during high school. We were untouched by genocide but somehow we were touched by its existence.

We had all prepared ideas to try out. I offered one of my favourite games; a task-based game in which every number called out is associated with an action that must be performed. The 8 numbers in our game represented the 8 stages of genocide and we were to collectively find an action to represent each stage. I suggested we look for everyday actions to associate with the atrocities described in the 8 stages.

Something in me was cringing as I explained the task. This game is playful, it is often used as a warm up, a fun activity. How on earth could we be playful with this material?

We brainstormed ideas and some of our free associations were:

classification: a bored librarian, queuing, athletes on a podium, a scientist in action, an entomologist pinning butterflies, school children in a line from shorter to taller...

symbolisation: anchovies, Star of David, long coat, high heels, big dog on a lead, hoodies, tattoos...

dehumanisation: looking through the garbage for food, pointing at someone, fancy dress party, a robotic supermarket assistant at the till...

organisation: tidying up, people pouring out of tube station at Canary Wharf, someone working in an abattoir, an administrator going through folders, wearing a uniform...

polarisation: blue and red teams, Apartheid, Romeo and Juliet, magnets, falling in love...

preparation: chopping onions, priming a canvas, getting ready for a wedding, rehearsing a speech in front of a mirror, bulldozers clearing land, a high jump athlete before jumping...

extermination: killing bugs with spray, setting an ants' nest on fire, killing flies, people queuing for gas chambers, teenagers killing their classmates, rat poison...

denial: a kid saying "I didn't break it!", Lefebvrian bishops denying the holocaust, white supremacist Eugene Terreblanche, denying the existence of aboriginal people around the world, a woman not believing that her boyfriend is cheating on her, not dealing with mourning...

We kept oscillating between enthusiasm and rejection of the material we were generating throughout the process, but that day we began to embody it and to some extent play with it. There is no theatre making without playfulness and this project is no different.

The task game ended up becoming our rehearsal warm up (it evolved from 8 to 10 stages after the document was amended by Genocide Watch). And it is always fun.

We gave ourselves permission to be playful with the material, to be trivial, to laugh about it, as this was the only way we could make theatre with it. It was also the only way we could deflect the weight of addressing a deeply saddening theme. We had to be able to joke about it and to transform the feelings of powerlessness and anger into creative exploration.

Playfulness requires readiness and presence, as opposed to pain and trauma that are disempowering feelings that block you and make you want to crawl under the duvet and never get out. We didn't want anyone to have this experience watching our show. Instead we wanted people to discuss, to think, to have agency, and our tool is to engage them in a playful experiment of theatre.

The Rag Factory
May 2014

2013

NINA NINA NINA NINA NINA NINA NINA NINA NINA NINA NIN

DEBORA DEBORA DEBORA DEBORA DEBORA DEB

MARCO MARCO MARCO MARCO MARCO MARCO

MAURO MAURO MAURO

ALI ALI ALI ALI ALI ALI

MEADHBH

GENEVIEVE GEI

LIZZIE LIZZIE LI

JEN JEN JEN JE

IRENE IRENE IR

BAC Scratch   WorkShops RAG Factory

2016

NINA NINA NINA NINA NINA NINA NINA NINA NINA NINA

DEBORA DEBORA DEBORA DEBORA DEBORA DEBORA DEBO

GENEVIEVE GENEVIEVE GENEVIEVE GENEVIEVE GENEVIE

LIZZIE LIZZIE LIZZIE LIZZIE LIZZIE LIZZIE LIZZIE LIZZIE LIZZIE

JEN JEN JEN JEN JEN JEN JEN JEN JEN JEN JEN JEN JEN JEN

IRENE IRENE IRENE IRENE IRENE IRENE IRENE IRENE IREN

ANDY ANDY ANDY ANDY ANDY ANDY ANDY ANDY AN

CAROLIN CAROLIN CAROLIN

SHANA SHAN

Theatre Delicatessen Performances   **To Date**

The Atmosphere of Genocide
Andreas Philippopoulos-Mihalopoulos

it began innocently and i got pulled in by it [1]

A simple question that usually gets a simple answer: do you like anchovies? This is the first distinction, the one that carves the universe into two: anchovy eaters and non-eaters. The theatre show begins deceptively innocently. The question hides nothing behind it. It is served on a platter of smiles and gentle but firm gestures.

But every distinction can call itself the first distinction[2]. Arian versus Jews, Jews versus Arabs, Christians versus others, ISIS versus others: we are all, at any point in time, part of multiple distinctions. Yet, we are, at any one point, dwellers of only one side. You cannot both eat and not-eat anchovies. To dwell on one side is natural, expected, legitimate, human – it is acceptable. The question is: what do you do about the other side?

a sense of inevitability

The curtain is drawn. Anchovy eaters are a lower breed of people. Convincing arguments are aired with the levity of factual information. When science is talking, the rest of us remain silent. Please do not take it personally. You need our help, and we can help. We create this world for you (and for us), for your benefit (and for ours), for your wellbeing (and for ours). This world is the distinction. There is an inside, and an outside, and nothing else. Nowhere else to go. There is no real outside: there are just two places, either side of the distinction, small bleeding universes of one asphyxiating atmosphere, brimming with affects that are in the service of the distinction.

Affects are senses: the anchovy-eaters were asked to don a sparkling little badge, which turned out to be a real anchovy, taxidermically elaborated but still carrying its full affect of fish smell. Affects are symbols: you on this side of the room, we on the other; distance please, no crossings; kneel down, return to the floor where you belong. Affects are emotions: do not pity them, you are superior; do not feel hard done: you are simply not good enough and you need to be helped. Affects are directed towards specific goals: we want you to see the other side for what it is. Anchovy-eaters: wallow in your inferiority, do not move beyond your assigned territory, do not remove your badge. Non-anchovy eaters: why would you want to cross? You have everything you need here. You belong here, amongst your peers. Look at that sorry lot and feel fortunate in your destiny. The affects are centripetally directed towards that all-devouring distinction. This is the inevitable distinction of the atmosphere.

they deprived me of the opportunity to think for myself

An atmosphere is the excess of affect that keeps bodies together, through and against each other[3]. The atmosphere at *No Feedback* is keeping the bodies together (on either side of the distinction) and separate (through the distinction). An atmosphere is an attractive thing, surrounding the earth, nestling in air-conditioned shopping malls, in fortress Europe, in our own little property fences. Atmosphere attracts but also excludes: it burns everything that crosses into its periphery unless designated to be part of the atmosphere. If accepted, you will be safe, cared for, helped: you will find your rightful, just position.

An atmosphere is regularly engineered in order to allocate and maintain pre-determined positions for each body. Every body knows its place and is expected to maintain it. Even if you second-guess, you remain. Nazi atmospheric engineering is one of the most immediately perceptible ones. There are others that are less so. Whatever they end up being, they often start as simple distinctions in terms of taste, origin, class, neighbourhood, sexuality, gender, race, religion. At their most innocent, they remain everyday distinctions of which each one of us tries to make sense, hesitating to accept them yet often indulging them. At their most brutal, they become genocidal atmospheres, where the other side must perish. There is a sense of threat coming from the other side, always perpetrated within by letting the door ajar, the curtain translucent, the bodies in relief: we need to be reminded of the blacks outside our gated community/the refugees outside our European borders/ the poor outside our tennis clubs. And there is a sense of wholeness perpetrated inside, a sticking-together in the face of the threat from the outside. Boundaries become more important than ever, exclusion becomes the only mechanism of self-preservation, and the world is ravaged once again with multiple distinctions lacerating its skin. We are victims of our own desires. We think we can think for ourselves but instead we have deferred our thinking to the atmosphere.

although the barrier was removed, it felt like a barrier was still there

But why not rebel? Why not move against the atmosphere? Because atmosphere builds on your and my desire to feed the atmosphere itself. Its greatest triumph is the fact that it uses our affects and our desires in order to maintain itself. A perfect thing, striving for its own perseverance, a perverse Spinozan conatus that aspires to become One, God, Nature: the Whole all-ingesting sphere of holy perfection, where all bodies are assigned positions in an inescapable theological pyramid. An atmosphere exists because we maintain it. They are fragile things, difficult to engineer fully, brittle to the touch, unpredictable. But they are also remarkably resourceful because they build on our bodies and our affects and feed on our own fears and desires.

A successfully engineered atmosphere fortifies itself by including conflict, gestures of going against it, even its own disruption. This is the total atmosphere: there is no outside and no real way out. Even when the atmosphere withdraws, like the barrier between our bodies, the barrier remains, folded in our desires. We are all, eaters and non-eaters, part of the atmosphere, serving it through our desire to remain. We are the atmosphere.

[1] The section titles are taken by the anonymous audience feedback sheets that were carried out after each performance.

[2] G. Spencer Brown, Laws of Form, London: George Allen and Unwin, 1969

[3] A. Philippopoulos-Mihalopoulos, Spatial Justice: Body, Lawscape, Atmosphere, London: Routledge, 2014

The Physicality of the Pink Lady Puppets
Irène Wernli

The questions around an individual's responsibility within the stages that can lead to genocide informed our search for a performative movement language. Our aim was to somehow manifest the intricate ambiguity of the subject. This posed a challenging task which we explored through improvisation. We kept returning to what we call 'human-puppetry', where one performer is animated and manipulated by another like a puppet. This way of working in partnership evoked very specific imagery with two very different and clearly defined roles: the inanimate or manipulated 'human puppet' read as the role of the innocent and passive. The active role of the puppeteer undoubtedly indicated a superior force. Initially sceptical about settling for a language that might be too literal or too familiar to audiences, we recognised the rich and bold kind of storytelling that this 'type of puppetry' would offer. The interdependence of the two roles meant that all of the actions had to be executed together. We started to play with the balance of power by creating movement material that allowed us to consistently swap roles within a pair. With these sequences we hope to touch upon the blurred lines of assigning blame and taking responsibility.

The continuing development of our own methodology of 'human puppetry' allows us to deepen the listening and the understanding of our own and our partner's body. We focus on initiations of movement, modes of impulse and reaction and the techniques of how to move together with confidence in a compliant and relaxed way. To me, the puppetry language has become a strong feature of the work, contributing a darkly funny layer and absurdity to the performance.

Lizzie Sells

place

No Feedback has been created by a group of artists working in London and wanting to tackle the issue of genocide from its most immediate surroundings. Despite periodical occurrences like Enoch Powell's "Rivers of Blood" speech, white nationalism of the National Front during the late 1970's or recent outbursts of Islamophobia from the British government and mass-media, the UK praises itself for its political, religious and cultural tolerance. Yet it is obvious that tolerance is all too fragile. It needs to be nurtured or it withers. As JG Ballard said of his own literary endeavours: "nothing is as secure as we like to think it is. A large part of my fiction tries to analyse what is going on around us, and whether we are much different people from the civilized human beings we imagine ourselves to be". This is the challenge that we set ourselves to examine: The fragility of tolerance within a precise socio-historical context of a sanitized, cosmopolitan city.

Many of the elements of the performance including props, script, location and even the performers themselves (six women of various nationalities) are representative of a precise time and place. As we prepare to tour the show this year, questions arise around symbolism and representation. Will our references to anchovies still seem humorous? Will the army of Stepford Wives resonate as eerie? Will a group of women considered diverse in one context be seen as homogenous elsewhere? The answers to all of these questions are explored when No Feedback is performed outside of London. Even if a performance responds to a precise environment, we are addressing a social phenomenon of universal implications. We continue to witness how a social experiment experienced as a theatrical event plays out in different cultures and with diverse publics.

space

As well as geographical and cultural context, I consider the micro spaces where *No Feedback* has emerged to have had a significant impact on the work over the years. We didn't have (or perhaps didn't want to have) access to traditional theatre environments, making use of whatever spaces we found available to us. One of our first partners, the Centre for Postcolonial Studies at Goldsmiths, University of London, provided us with large classrooms in which to work. The institutional nature of these rooms did not feel at odds with the nature of the material we were generating; 'educational', pseudo-scientific speeches that would be preached to the audience, physical languages to communicate organisation and establishment. Our first performances happened on the first floor of the Rag Factory space in East London. This was a dirty, dusty and uncomfortable room that seemed to fit the strange, dystopian quality of the work we had created. As we weren't in a conventional theatre and had provided nowhere for the audience to sit (other than on the floor) the makeshift and unpolished nature of the Rag Factory demanded the audience make a series of choices from the moment they arrived. The individuals' reaction to the space was crucial in understanding their responses to the piece. Each night the public reacted differently to the situation they found themselves in. For that very reason, we ended up improvising alternative endings for the show depending on how people behaved during the performance.

This notion of how a space is presented and its potential to effect experience is critical to how *No Feedback* is encountered. Generally speaking, spaces within museums or memorials of genocide try to evoke the atmosphere of events that once happened there. Two examples are the Tuol Sleng Museum in Cambodia and the Higher School of Mechanics of the Navy, the infamous ESMA in Buenos Aires. Both places restage interior and exterior spaces as they would have been during the period of their use as prisons and extermination centres. The effect is a visceral theatre-cum-museum where the visitor can come closer to tragedy by experiencing first hand the horrors that still haunt these buildings. However, such performativity of space is exactly what *No Feedback* seeks to avoid. We are not interested in creating a dystopian environment, perhaps expected from a performance about genocide. It is the commonplace, everyday space that hosts the work best. In such a mundane environment the actions and reactions of the audience are what create their experience and crucially lines between the theatrical and real worlds become blurred.

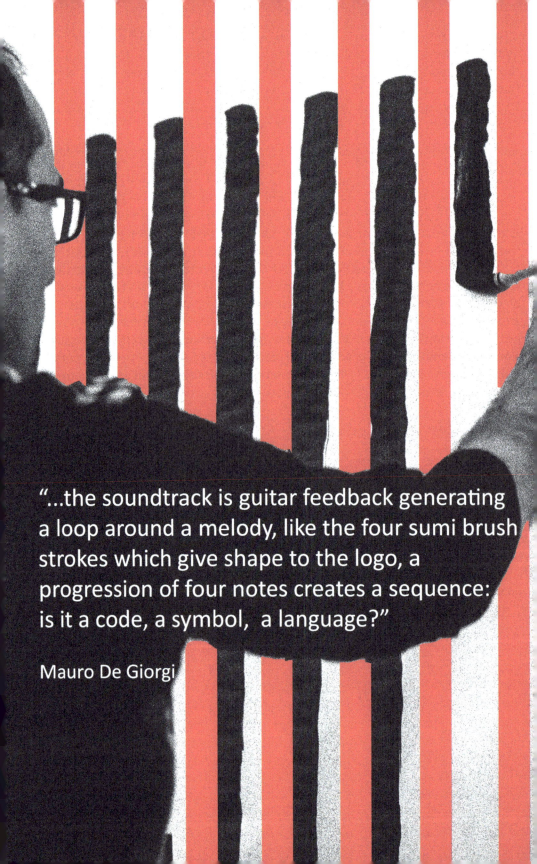

"...the soundtrack is guitar feedback generating a loop around a melody, like the four sumi brush strokes which give shape to the logo, a progression of four notes creates a sequence: is it a code, a symbol, a language?"

Mauro De Giorgi

On Empathy

Jen Plants

I've been taught (and in interests of full disclosure, I often teach to others) that theatre making follows this equation: actor + idea + audience = theatre. It seems simple, right? An actor (someone with a body) performs an idea (which is often a script) for an audience (who by definition are the hearers, the seers, the receivers.) However, this equation makes performances where the body of the actor transmits the idea of someone else (traditionally, a playwright,) and the audience simply observes, no matter how emotionally or intellectually engaged they may be. After some transformative experiences making work in out of the way places (a loft in an old barn in upstate New York, a former folk high school in Denmark,) I couldn't help but wonder what would happen if the role of the audience could be activated to the point that their experience was the key in the equation, not simply their existence. Perhaps the idea of an equation itself is the problem, as you can't quantify experience, and after all, the whole point of live performance thrives on the intangible.

As an actor myself trained in traditional stage work, my first professional role after graduate school was in a contemporary play about the 1990's Bosnian genocide. The performing ensemble was made up of all women (just like No Feedback) and the subject of violent forms of discrimination was another commonality, but the style and purpose could not have been more starkly different. Through scenes of emotional realism, the play about Bosnia was designed to provoke catharsis, not action. Performers re-enacted suffering that was co-opted from the lived experiences of others in order to tell a cohesive story to an American audience. This very "re-enaction" puts audiences at a distance. You may observe and feel this "real" story from the past portrayed with skill by trained actors, but you are not invited to embody or act as you sit quietly in the audience observing. A particularly strong performance that meets an audience member at just the right moment in time may have invited emotional empathy and tears during curtain call, but ultimately, the audience is simply the receiver and the actors the only transmitters.

My role in the production set in Bosnia was emotionally explosive, and my last gut-wrenching scene was the penultimate scene in the play. I spent the last several minutes of each production before curtain call backstage stress-eating puffed cheese balls and wondering if those in the audience were moved as I was. We use the idea of being "moved" in the theatre as moving from one emotional place to another, but the irony of the term is that no one in the audience is moving much at all. Looking back, I realize now that what I longed for then was to provide the audience with an experience of applied empathy (as defined by Director of Movement at Northern Illinois University Heather L. Corwin): the ability to reach into another's experience and feel it personally without judgment. And there's the key: without judgment. Inviting the audience to simply observe invites pity--which can be a step on the way to compassion, but is really inherently a judgement as pity requires that you see yourself as better off than another. "Oh those poor people in Bosnia! What suffering they endured." These thoughts might make you cry, but they don't invite action or perspective shifting--you still see everything through your own eyes and the point of view you had when you walked through the theatre door.

Alternatively, immersive performances allow the audience to be active in body as well as mind. Audiences can interrogate the "text" from multiple angles by moving themselves, rather than relying on the vantage point of the seat they were able to afford. Spectacle itself can become a kind of text, rather than a separate element simply designed to support literal language. Immersive performances engage all the senses--you literally find your whole self a part of something moving, rather than waiting to be moved. In No Feedback, the audience is guided through an experience that they--in many ways--create themselves--by playing games, forming alliances and divisions, and making choices (whether they realize that there are choices to be made or not.) Without a text imported from a recent hit in London or New York (or a dead man from Stratford), each audience member situates the imagined world of the performance within their own experience. For me, as an American in this current moment, the performance is about institutional racism (but the number of contexts others have seen in No Feedback's strange world of pink ladies is the stuff of another article.) You can't then think, "Oh those poor people!" when examining a first-person experience.

Personal sensory experiences move empathetic responses from a private act where the intellect meets the emotions to a performed action where feelings must be embodied. In No Feedback, a constant stream of rules, boundaries, activities and movement distracts the self from judgment, which leads to the possibility of applied empathy. Taken one step further, the experience of applied empathy can invite you to perform actions in response to a new perspective. So, when applied empathy is activated in an audience, the audience acts. Who is transmitting and receiving now?

At No Feedback's conception, one of the central questions was what does genocide have to do with an average Londoner today? How can a performance connect people across culture, language and experience without "othering"? Whether you are traveling to work, grabbing a bite to eat, hugging a loved one, or tripping on the sidewalk, you are performing actions and encountering others every day. Only lack of awareness prevents performed actions in life from having greater meaning. Calling attention to our performances in a confined space and time creates meaning from an audience's experiences and actions. Combine that with the performing ensemble and the disconcerting world of No Feedback, and you have an invitation to apply empathy to others. "Oh those poor people," no longer applies when those people are us.

In No Feedback, everyone in the room is "us," and that old equation of actor + audience + idea starts to break down, particularly as it splits the actor and the audience into two separate and distinct components. After a No Feedback performance, I don't find myself wanting to stress eat alone in a hallway, wondering if anyone out there in the house was "moved" or not (which is an "us" and "them" scenario if there ever was one,) because we have all moved--together. The audience is as much a transmitter of the ideas of the show as I am, and we share an experience. Perspective taking happens through our own eyes, our own experience, which we connect to the experience of others, and. . . well, that's empathy. We've reached into another's experience and felt it personally without judgment, and if there is to be a revolution in human understanding, there is no better place to start.

Parched Anchovies and Feather Ticklers
Marco Monterzino

As an industrial designer I felt that my contribution to *No Feedback* would fall somewhere between concept and materiality. I have an interest in collaborative practice and working on this project was a great chance to learn how to negotiate the sensitive topic of genocide as a team. When I wrote my own brief to start making sense of the journey ahead, I was led to an initial hypothesis: through the bodily experience of tangible performative objects each audience member would be an empowered autonomous agent in the world of the show.

As a team we discussed the narrative and shared our frames of reference for the making of the performance. Reading from my early sketches <<One group hates the other for the most deliberately mundane and absurd reason: anchovy eating >>. To classify the participating audience and facilitate the "us and them" situation we used a tangible device. I designed an identification brooch, a seductive jewel made from the parched carcass of an anchovy, a golden brooch pin mounted through black lining and encrusted with six iridescent crystals. When we tested it during a scratch performance, only the anchovy eaters received one to wear, leaving the rest of the audience empty-handed.

For the further development of the material aspects of the performance I started investigating the issue of geographical distance between us and the actual topic of our research. In order to explore that as a team we used a design probe. I created a set of psychogeographical drift kits comprising a sealable sachet, a twin-layer folded map, a coloured pencil and a set of actions. When we tested it in Canary Wharf we aimed to drift from the everyday experience of the built environment by creating a set of situations. To treasure the insights from our exercise, we reacted to the experience in the languages of our own practices.

I went back to the drawing board with a view to creating a new kit for our audiences to become constructors of situations themselves. The new kit contained a number of tools of scientific fiction. A pen-sized bamboo handle crowned with soft feathers, bound together with a brass filament was a tool for the production of pleasure, the tickler. It was designed to create interplay between two participating members of the audience, one stroking the other's most sensitive part of the neck to measure the degree of pleasure on a Visual Analogue Scale.

It has been a fascinating collaborative journey which I am happy to have learned from and contributed to. Thanks to the multidisciplinary nature of the project I have been able to push the boundaries of my practice as a designer and it gave me a chance to appreciate how the team members' diverse skill sets were complementary in many ways. In conclusion I feel that the initial hypothesis was confirmed and that the design of performative artefacts has contributed to the collaborative effort towards the empowerment of the audience.

Trials as Theatre: A Case Study

What follows are excerpts from a talk given by Dr. Daniela Nadj as part of a 2015 No Feedback-associated event. Nadj is a Lecturer in Public Law and the Course Convenor in Administrative Law at Queen Mary University of London, as well as a member of the Centre for Law and Society in a Global Context (CLSGC.)

"War doesn't end with the last bullet" -- Chiseche S. Mibenge

What is the price of inclusion? How can the wrongs of the past be remedied? Can they ever be remedied?

The aim of this piece is to bring to light the account of victims, witnesses, survivors, perpetrators, those who saw and lived through armed conflict, told in international criminal tribunals, with a particular focus on the International Criminal Tribunal for Rwanda (ICTR).

The term genocide "is a modern word for an old crime". The UN General Assembly eventually promulgated a multilateral treaty defining the crime of genocide (Article II of the Convention on the Prevention and Punishment of the Crime of Genocide 1948) as follows:

In the present Convention, genocide means any of the following acts committed with the intent to destroy, in whole or in part, a national, ethnical, racial or religious group, as such:

- Killing members of the group;
- Causing serious bodily or mental harm to members of the group;
- Deliberately inflicting on the group conditions of life calculated to bring about its physical destruction in whole or in part;
- Imposing measures intended to prevent births within the group;
- Forcibly transferring children of the group to another group.

The definition has been incorporated verbatim into the statutes of the ad hoc international criminal tribunals for Yugoslavia and Rwanda set up in 1993 and 1994 in the wake of the armed conflict in the Former Yugoslavia and the genocide in Rwanda, respectively.

The people of Rwanda (and Burundi) descended from three distinct populations: one known as the Hutu, who resembled the Bantu people of the region; and the second, the Tutsi, who resembled Cushitic or Nilotic people in the Horn of Africa; and third, the Twa, related to the local pigmy populations. Over time, these groups intermixed and developed a common language and culture.

During the colonial era, from approximately 1890 to 1962, Belgian colonial administrators solidified these distinctions by "assigning" individuals an "ethnicity" on a state-issued identity card. The Hutu represented about eighty-four percent of the population, the Tutsi constituted about fifteen percent, and the Twa about one percent. Rwanda achieved its independence in 1962 under the leadership of the.

Belgium-installed Gregoire Kayibanda, a Hutu leader, who imposed ethnically-based quotas for access to schools, some industries and the civil service that significantly limited Tutsi participation in these sectors. The victory of Hutu parties increased the departure of Tutsi to neighbouring countries from where Tutsi exiles made incursions into Rwanda. The word 'Inyenzi', meaning cockroach, came to be used to refer to these assailants.

In 1994, thousands of people, sometimes encouraged, or directed by local administrative officials, on the promise of safety, gathered unsuspectingly in churches, schools, hospitals and local government buildings. In reality, this was a trap intended to lead to the rapid extermination of a large number of people. The killings of Tutsi, which from then on spared neither women nor children, continued up to July 18, 1994, when the Rwandan Patriotic Front (RFP) triumphantly entered Kigali. The estimated total number of victims in the conflict varies from 500,000 to 1,000,000 or more.

In 1997, the landmark ICTR decision, The Prosecutor v. Akayesu, was the first case that ever combined the notion that acts of rape and other forms of sexual violence could be charged as genocide-in addition to crimes against humanity and war crimes.

The primary allegations against Jean-Paul Akayesu were not that he personally engaged in acts of violence, but that as a mayor of the Taba commune he had superior or command responsibility for those serving under his watch. He was therefore charged with ordering, inciting, or instigating international war crimes, crimes against humanity and genocide. As one witness described it, "Akayesu did not kill with his own hands, but with his orders."

Specifically, Akayesu was individually charged with genocide, complicity in genocide, extermination, murder, torture, cruel treatment, rape, other inhumane acts and outrages upon personal dignity, which he allegedly committed in Rwanda's Taba commune.

The victims referred to in Akayesu's indictment were persons not taking active part in the hostilities. The judgment and the transcripts of the trial reveal that the majority of civilian casualties were women. To call armed conflict "armed" in contemporary international legal discourses is misleading because the civilian hostages targeted for enslavement, amputation, mutilation, rape, torture, abduction, summary execution, forced labour, and other gross violations of human rights are for the most part unarmed.

It is these stories that need to be told. Courtroom witness, Dr. Mathias Ruzindana, noted that most Rwandans live in an oral tradition in which facts are reported as they are perceived by the witness, often irrespective of whether the facts were personally witnessed, or recounted by someone else. Since a large percentage of Rwandans were illiterate, but owned radios, much of the hate propaganda against the Tutsi in 1994 was transmitted through the radio and by word of mouth.

Allegations of sexual violence first came to the attention of the Chamber through the testimony of Witness J, a Tutsi woman, who was six months pregnant at the time. Most of her family members had been killed by militia at her home. J and her six year-old daughter managed to escape this fate by hiding in a tree and scavenging for food. In response to questioning from the Prosecutor, witness J suddenly mentioned:

"My six year-old daughter has been raped by three Interahamwe when they came to kill her father late in the evening. She screamed and cried throughout and her screams are still piercing my ears. I heard that young girls were raped at the bureau communal. They didn't spare a single one of them!"

It transpired that she had never been questioned about this by any investigators of the Tribunal.

If J had not offered the fact that her six-year old daughter had been raped, the existence of sexual violence in Taba commune might have never made it into the formal record.

The Indictment was amended to include allegations of sexual violence and additional charges against the Accused. Suddenly, we see a decisive shift in the courtroom dynamic. The following testimonies given after the amendment to the indictment illustrate the shift in focus away from male murder victims to female victims of wartime sexual violence.

Witness OO, a young Tutsi woman describes the events:

"Me and my family sought refuge at the bureau communal in April 1994 and we saw many other Tutsi refugees there, on the road outside the compound. Some Interahamwe arrived and started killing people with machetes. Two other girls and I tried to flee but we were stopped by the Interahamwe. They went back and told Akayesu that they were taking the girls away to "sleep with" them. I was standing five meters away from Akayesu and I heard him say: "take them!" I was then separated from the other girls and taken to a field by one Interahamwe called Antoine. When I refused to sit down, he pushed me to the ground and put his "sex" into mine. I mean he penetrated my vagina with his penis! When I started to cry, he warned me that if I cried or shouted, others might come and kill me."

Witness KK, a Hutu woman married to a Tutsi man:

"My husband was beaten at the bureau communal and injured on the head. He escaped, but he was captured by the Interahamwe. I received a message from him. He wanted to speak to me before he died. I found him behind the bureau communal with Interahamwes armed with clubs and spears, who then took him away between the two buildings of the bureau communal. I learned later that he was killed. I later went to Akayesu and asked him for an attestation to help me keep my children alive. He replied that it was not he who had made them be born Tutsi and that:

"When rats are killed you don't spare rats that are still in the form of a fetus!"

"I was pregnant and miscarried after being beaten by police and Interahamwe. Of my nine children, only two survived the events."

"I saw women and girls selected and taken away to the cultural center at the bureau communal by Interahamwes. They said they were going to "sleep with" these women and girls. Akayesu told the Interahamwe to undress a young girl named Chantal, whom he knew to be a gymnast, so that she could do gymnastics naked. Akayesu told Chantal, who said she was Hutu, that she must be a Tutsi because he knew her father to be a Tutsi. Chantal was forced to march around naked in front of many people. Akayesu was laughing and happy with this. He told the Interahamwes to take her away and said:

"You should first of all make sure that you sleep with this girl."

The Defence alluded to the fragility of human testimony as opposed to documentary evidence, whilst denying individual criminal responsibility for the sexual violence committed against women in the Taba commune.

In its 169-page judgement, the Tribunal found Akayesu liable for inciting, ordering, and causing harm to Tutsi individuals seeking refuge in the bureau communal. He was convicted of murder, extermination, and torture as crimes against humanity. In relation to the acts of sexual violence, through ordering, instigating, or aiding and abetting these acts, Akayesu was found guilty of the crimes against humanity of rape and "other inhumane acts". In so doing, the Chamber for the first time defined rape and sexual violence under international law from a conceptual perspective. "Like torture, rape is a violation of personal dignity, and rape in fact constitutes torture when it is inflicted by or at the instigation of or with the acquiescence of a public official, or other person acting in an official capacity."

On the genocide counts, the Tribunal found that Akayesu acted with genocidal intent, and that genocide had occurred in Rwanda. It also explicitly recognised the concept of 'genocidal rape', when it ruled that the acts of rape and sexual violence in the record could serve as predicate acts of genocide along with the other murders and assaults on members of the Tutsi group.

The Tribunal concluded that even those rapes that do not result in the death of the victim could constitute genocide, where "sexual violence was a step in the process of the destruction of the Tutsi group-destruction of the spirit, of the will to live, and of life itself."

At the same time, it recognised that the goal of many acts of sexual violence was to make Tutsi women suffer and to mutilate them even before killing them, the intent being to destroy the Tutsi group in whole or in part, while inflicting acute suffering on its members in the process. In this way, the Tribunal emphasised that both mental and physical harm associated with rape satisfied the actus reus of the crime of genocide.

Akayesu was convicted of genocide. He was given a life sentence, his appeal was rejected, with several other defendants he was transported to Bamako, Mali, where he is serving a life sentence following an agreement between that country and the Tribunal. To this day, the Akayesu is seen as the landmark case on wartime sexual violence in international law having transformed the perceptions of the international community about the gendered experience of wartime for women.

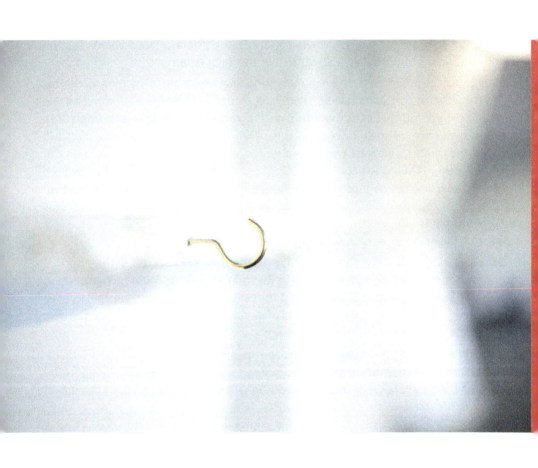

Resisting Genocidal Forces

Shana Swiss

After two decades of working with women in countries undergoing genocidal conflicts, I was curious and intrigued when I learned about a performance that used the 10 Stages of Genocide as its skeletal framework. I wondered how a 60-minute theatrical experience could translate horrific crimes and powerful resistance into a creative form that would provoke the discovery of what allows, and then holds in place, the discrimination and hatred that fuels these atrocities.

And yet, as a former dancer and dance therapist, I know first hand the surprise, the delight, the power and the insight that can come from the creation of both verbal and non-verbal stories. Fictional stories capture our imagination—they take us out of our known reality. Difficult emotions can be experienced from a more creative angle. Metaphor can allow an exploration with more playfulness and less shame.

As an audience member for the premiere of *No Feedback* in London, I was amazed at how this participatory performance piece could provoke the kind of self-discovery that leads to action. In the days following the performance, I noticed how I had changed when encountering a situation of "othering"—even though I have been an activist for many years. I was so surprised at this that I went back to see the performance again—to make sure that participating in a single performance could initiate that kind of change.

When I realized the powerful potential that *No Feedback* has to promote the kind of self-discovery that leads to real behavioral change, I knew that I wanted to work with the Company to take *No Feedback* out of the theatre and into universities and communities.

I have worked for over two decades with local groups in situations of armed conflict. As a public health physician, I have watched the transformative process that occurs when people link their own knowledge and self-discovery with action to change their lives and communities. I have been so inspired by the creativity, courage and stubborn hope of people in the midst of armed conflict that the only way I could collaborate with them was to engage in a problem-posing approach that honors their knowledge and practice. I have used methods of popular education that begin with reflection on the women's life experience as the basis for learning and that enables them to develop a social analysis of the causes of war, conflict, and their own disempowered position as women. Stories, plays, and discussions about their daily lives confirm their authority as community members who know their problems and can find solutions that work.

It seems to me that this model could be used to support the kind of discovery-based learning that encourages people to reflect critically upon their world and allows them to break the "culture of silence" that leads to numbness and indifference, and that mobilizes them to try out new behaviors that challenge discrimination and inequities.

In partnership with the No Feedback Company and the People's Palace Projects, an Arts for Social Change organisation at Queen Mary University London, a pilot is being developed that supports local versions of *No Feedback* to be adapted by amateur actors in universities and communities. University students and community members will engage in a process that encourages an exploration of the ways that we collude to exclude people and how the process of "othering" leads to a host of social problems in our communities, from bullying and hate crimes to violent extremism. The "local" performers could become leaders in their own communities and through an iterative process develop another team of local actors. This model of grassroots leadership replication fosters growth and sustainability.

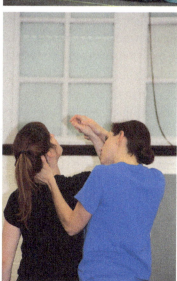

The Challenge of Creating a Character for No Feedback

Carolin Ott

The beauty of creating a character for *No Feedback* is freedom. With it come challenges that have to be thought about and well prepared. First of all there isn't a script. Well, there is one, but if you think about a script in a traditional sense then this isn't it. There are no character names. No stage directions. No Beginning. Middle. End. Instead, we have sections or chapters if you like to think of that way and those push our story forward.

I was thrown into this piece and very quickly had to establish a voice, physicality and an emotional connection to both of my characters, which was equally scary and freeing. As a Classically and Lecoq trained actress, I am used to spending a substantial amount of time doing text work and also devising from scratch. The text that we use sets a tone and foundation for our work which we can then play around with to determine the overall journey of the piece. When I prepare a character, I usually read the script several times and note down first impressions, such as words my character repeatedly says, do they talk a lot, who do they talk to most of the time, what do other people say about them, do I get an idea of the quality of vocal pace, volume from the words etc. I also like writing back stories and creating a three dimensional character- the more I know about the character, the better I can portray them. Questions I would ask myself are: Who am I? Where have I just come from? What do I want? I like making bold choices, thinking outside the box and getting things up on their feet to establish a sense of a being. As mentioned above, there are no character names in *No Feedback* and one of my roles is the Pink Lady. A Hostess. An employee, merely doing her job. An overenthusiastic puppeteer of a faceless worker who becomes a tool, delivering the message. How do you puppeteer a human with no strings? This was a fantastic opportunity to make unique choices, especially physically. The Pink Lady never looks at participants, she uses her voice and puppet to communicate and give instructions. The puppet is lifeless. Almost like a slave of society and as a performer I had to get used to letting go completely and to follow the impulses of my puppeteer, who on the other hand seems to be towering over me, using my body as a platform to get across what she has been told to tell.

The challenge of creating a character for *No Feedback* is that it is an immersive show, the audience are part of it and every performance is different. Right from the beginning the Pink Ladies welcome and almost entice the audience into a bleak space of the unknown and lay out the rules of our meeting. The audience becomes a device and must adhere to orders otherwise there will be consequences. The Pink Lady sees the audience member as a participant, a member of the public who is taking part in the meeting in order to learn and be educated. So she hosts to the best of her ability, makes sure that no one steps out of line and is ready to take control if she needs to. She does not seek conversation. She seeks only to fulfill

46

the requirements of her job. This makes the relationship between the audience and the Pink Ladies an artificial one, that in the end vanishes. In terms of character development, not only did I have to know how my character would react in certain situations, but we also had to build an ensemble that collaborates strongly, listens and most importantly trusts.

The text that we are working with is currently 7 pages long. A showing is usually around 60 minutes in length. And half the lines are pre-recorded. Can you guess what I am about to say?

You.

The audience are such a big part of this endeavour. This is why it is so much fun for us, the performers. We are there to guide you through the show or as we call it 'the meeting' and offer you an unforgettable experience. An experience where you have a voice within our world. As a performer, my character's thoughts must become my first language, I have to have tricks up my sleeve, a tool box to be used, think on my feet and be ready to improvise. This, to me, was creative freedom. To share a space with a group of people and experience a push and pull of events that could take us in many different directions. To watch your every move, to make you think and listen to what you have to say. Giving thought to the subject matter of this piece, your voice will most likely be loud and audible.

Or silent.

I guess we started thinking the obvious, "militia".

But we didn't want to make it immediately obvious. We didn't want to be threatening, nor to induce a sense of hostility in the audience, at least not straightaway..

So we thought of an opposite, "nurses".

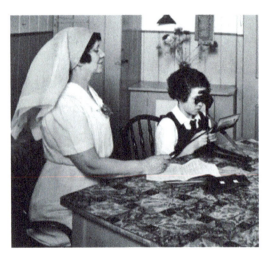

Nurses that will accompany the audience through scientific tests. They represent someone we would trust. Someone who is a professional in reassuring. Who we would generally follow even if we don't understand what is going on. And even if it might cause us pain.

Somehow very early on we thought "pink".

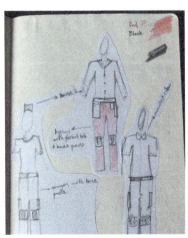

Our characters represent manipulation (we are manipulated, we manipulate others) and lack of responsibility (we follow orders). We are part of a machine that only occasionally reveals itself. But successful manipulation is sly and seductive. It presents itself as a solution as it leads you somewhere else.

So we thought " friendly, smile".

But we are a machine, we were using the language of puppeteering each other to represent a lack of will and a lack of humanity, repeating actions learned as part of our 'training'.

And then we thought "air hostesses"

Equally seductive and robotic, we found air hostesses weirdly hypnotic in their choreographed explanation of safety procedures. They are often wearing a mask of friendliness that is somehow unreal, nearly plastified.

(Some hostesses in airports are now holograms!)

Eventually we came across a video of the Chinese women's army and there it was, the perfect mix between a soldier and an air hostess, in pink.

That was the inspiration, but we had a ridiculously small budget, it is better to say we didn't have any budget at all···

So we hit a huge retail store at 7pm on a Saturday evening, hoping to find something we could work with. And we did, in the perfect shade of pink. We just needed a pocket in the dress, which we solved by inserting a sock inside the lateral seam.

We added white kneepads (militia), white plimsoles (nurse) and a white handkerchief around the neck (air hostess). We tried the hat, but realised its impracticality in a highly physical show. And we were ready for the first work in progress of the show at the Rag Factory.

The pink dresses became more and more important in the show, as we embraced the dissonance between their bright, somewhat cheap and girly aesthetic, and the message of discrimination that they bore. Sugar coated hate.

The Scientist and the Social Construction of Scientific Fact

Genevieve Maxwell

It is a dark, damp February afternoon, and I'm standing on the backs of two people slowly crawling forward whilst decreeing the scientifically proven beneficial qualities of anchovies. My entourage holds me in place with regal care, my metatarsals do a micro-dance moulded over the lower vertebrae of my compatriots as I harness my core strength, loosen my jaw and project to the imaginary crowds with absolute authority: *"We have vital, cutting-edge stem cell research to share with you tonight. Its revolutionary findings will improve the quality of your life...."* before I am lifted down, feet to earth and blend once more with the 'crowd'.

"The scientist can only speak when their feet are off the ground. The scientist can only be heard when 'society' is carrying them". During that audition on that rainy afternoon, a concept was being physicalized that I recognized, mentally and viscerally, instantly[1].

The tale of the construction of our Scientist character, sits unconsciously hand in hand with a tale of the construction of the multiple cultural narratives of the formation of science, and the social construction of scientific fact.

But science is truth, I hear you say! Indeed, in contemporary western society, science is often held up as the 'high priestess of truth', by which exciting, ground-breaking revelations about our well-being and ways of living are made, and upon which pivotal governmental decision making processes are often unquestioningly based. I will not refute the significance and marvelling mind-blowing nature of much of what science has to offer us. But, I'll take you on a little 'backstage tour' of this incredible knowledge-making industry...

laboratory life: science as human activity

We tend to assume that the pursuit of scientific knowledge is a precise and controlled process, one that involves detailed experiments, careful analysis, peer review and demonstrable evidence. But what if it's not as simple as that?

In 1979 Anthropologist and Sociologist duo Bruno Latour and Steve Woolgar spent two years observing daily life in a laboratory at The Salk Institute for Biological Studies, California[2]. Situating themselves as cultural outsiders, they treated the activities conducted in the lab with the same level of dispassion and fascination as they would an exotic tribe.

In identifying the production of papers as the main output of the scientific lab, they observed a system whereby statements go through a series of socially influenced micro-processes in a staged journey towards becoming a fact.

'Scientific facts' are devised in layers, accumulating to a crystallized 'fact' that becomes devoid of its original context of production. Within those layers, a surprising amount of human influence and subjective judgment takes place. Layers of transcription (graphs and diagrams), selection of which results to use, minor adjustments of 'p' values and re-framing of the evidence can continually shift the statement in a socio-culturally determined way. Each layer masks to a degree the process involved in the processing of the previous layer, until eventually a 'fact' is born.

How that fact fares in the wider world, and in relation to other facts, depends largely on who produced that fact and where it came from. Scientists value trust, since the time and money involved in reproducing experiments is impractical. Instead, 'credit' gained from studying at a particular institution, working at a particular lab, or with another scientist of repute, means the work is more likely to be cited and gain more credit in a spiralling process they label 'Cycles of Credit' - a process that ultimately privileges the narrative of some facts over others.

science today

Fast-forward to the science industry today, the commercial pressures on scientists to produce 'facts' have increased dramatically. Expected production of papers has gone up by 500%[3], whilst retractions due to fraud or error increased tenfold in first part of the 21st Century[4]. Since 'facts' only stand until falsified by further studies[5], the sheer volume of 'facts' and data being produced mean that many remain unchallenged[6]. Today's cycles of credit are gambled on a stock- exchange-like 'H-Index', measuring frequency of citations in desirable journals seeking 'exciting'[7] science stories of public interest. The scramble for funding and race to be published can lead to serious compromise in the data selected for testing[8], and the funding available- driven by current industrial and political interest- make for a less than objective means of production of 'truth'.

the science of genocide

Between 1922 and 1945, scientists came to Belgian ruled Rwanda to classify and measure the native population. Under previous German colonial rule, the Tutsi ruling class were proclaimed to be intellectually superior based on contemporary genetic theory, due to their taller, slenderer, more 'European' looks. Geneticists, Physicians and Anthropologists arrived in Rwanda to measure the skulls of the population- believing skull size was synonymous with the evolution of brain size and therefore intelligence. Since craniological tests proved the Tutsis' skulls were larger and their skin was lighter, scientists proclaimed them descended of Caucasian heritage and genetically superior to their Hutu counterparts. A history was written to justify the racial distinctions, and ethnicity cards were issued. The Tutsi began to believe their own myth, and, holding positions of local power, increased in wealth. And so was constructed a set of 'facts' which defined a fatal power imbalance which set the stage for a series of shifting power battles and mass genocide[9].

Between 1933 and 1945 the application of Darwinian concepts of evolution were applied to the perceived 'problems of human society' in a mass campaign to 'cleanse'

German society of individuals viewed as a 'biological threat' to the nation's health. This scientific theory of Eugenics (which had also gained notoriety and popularity throughout Europe and the U.S.) employed the services of physicians, Geneticists, Psychiatrists and Anthropologists, and resulted in 400,000 forced sterilizations, over 275,000 'euthanasia deaths'[10] and further led to the Holocaust and the extermination of some six million Jews and other ethnic minorities.

Euphemistically referred to at the time as 'Aryan Racial Hygiene', 'Medical Killing' or 'Bioethics', it is startling to wonder now how such theories came to be upheld as scientific theory. And yet, as historian Richard J. Evans denotes:

"...What is so disturbing is how prosaic the reality was; how similar in form, if not content their work has to the research of today.

....What scientists did under The Third Reich was regarded as 'normal science', subject to the standard protocols of peer review in conferences and journals. "[11]

Both are examples of how the trajectory of the construction of scientific fact came to be fatally intertwined with social and political narrative to disastrous consequence. And yet, both were thought to be 'normal science' in their time.

'our scientist'

Our 'scientist', or the mythological construct we call The Scientist in No Feedback, was born out of inspiration from previous genocides, in combination with a need for a dividing device that would arbitrarily divide a London audience today. In a case of art unconsciously mirroring life, we knew what desired outcome we were aiming for; and set our methodology accordingly. *"We basically needed a way to divide up the audience"* explains No Feedback founder Nina Feldman. *"We devised an equation: no audience goer is likely to voluntarily put themselves at the extreme end of a scale. So we literally ran figures through an equation to see what the results could be"* recalls co-founder Debora Minà.

There needed to be a symbol of division – something banal; something that people felt strongly that they either liked or disliked. The symbolism of the Anchovy was born early on in the process, and stuck- not least due to its multi-sensorial properties.

The physicalized character of The Scientist has been a subconscious Archaeology[12] of process. *"My memory of the seeds of The Scientist are predominantly physicalized memories- of an elevated person, taking up space"* explains Debora Minà. 'We started to imagine him/her being carried in a chair by a team of assistants or researchers who could provide The Scientist with everything (s)he needed'.

In devising The Scientist we have played with multiple variations of physicalized embodiment. We spent numerous afternoons choreographing complex lifts, and even a way for The Scientist to walk across the crowd- but in the end a much more simplified and mechanistic lift won-out. The repetition perhaps reminiscent of the repeated and mundane running (and alteration of) data as the narrative gradually accumulates in tone towards the climax of the show, where our 'scientist' blurs with the figure of a politician, propagandist and even preacher. As for who is speaking- we have found it to be most eerie and powerful when the voice of The Scientist comes from the ensemble. After all, scientific theory cannot live in a vacuum- it is rather a combined product of processing involving the multiple voices of institutions, funding bodies, publications and their audiences. Science needs to be believed in and upheld by society to thrive.

Calcium and Magnesium are contained in large amounts in anchovies, and are well documented to affect the expansion and contraction of muscles. The implications of that finding are far-reaching within the human body. I leave it up to you, the audience, to deduce where the extrapolation of theory crosses the line in to 'rogue science'.

[1] The social construction of scientific fact was a core theory in my previous studies in Medical Anthropology, and one I revisited later as an artist in Wellcome Trust funded Laboratory Life residency at The Lighthouse, Brighton in 2011, and Hong Kong Microwave Festival 2012.

[2] Latour, B & Woolgar, S (1979) *Laboratory Life: The Construction of Scientific Facts* Beverley Hills: Sage Publications

[3] Professor Mark Edwards Saving Science from the Scientists Episode 2 BBC Radio 4, 21st March 2016

[4] Professor Ivan Oransky *"Why has the number of scientific retractions increased?"* Retraction Watch, July 11th 2013. Available from www.Retractionwatch.com

[5] Gee, Henry (2013) *Science: The Religion that must not be questioned* The Guardian, 19th September 2013

[6] Puniewska, Maggie *"Scientists have a sharing problem"* The Atlantic, Washington December 15th 2014.

[7] Dr Marcia McNutt, Editor in Chief of Nature Journal. Cited in *Saving Science from the Scientists* Episode 2 BBC Radio 4, 21st March 2016.

[8] Latour & Woolgar (1979); Kuhn, Thomas (1962, 2012) *The Structure of Scientific Revolutions* University of Chicago Press; Dr Bishop, Dorothy *Ten Red Flags in Research Integrity: Don't let Transparency damage Science Nature,* 25th January 2016.

[9] Malkki, Liisa (1995) *Purity and Exile* University of Chicago Press

[10] Kuhl, Stefan (1994) *The Nazi Connection: Eugenics, American Racism and German National Socialism* Oxford University Press

[11] Evans, Richard J. (2009) *The Third Reich at War* London: Penguin Press

[12] Foucault, M (1969) *Archaeology of Knowledge* London & New York: Routledge

The Anatomy of No Feedback
Nina Feldman

No Feedback is a living, dynamic, personal monument to all those who have suffered at the hands of genocide. Here *No Feedback*'s founding member and performance artist, Nina Feldman, describes the impetus and creative methodology behind this new, insightful and above all important piece of immersive theatre.

Being brought up on South African political theatre that had a clear function in the liberation movement, I was trained to think in a certain way about artistic production. Why was the work being made? Who was it being made by? How was it being made? Who was it being made for?

No Feedback brings together a number of strands that have concerned me since beginning my creative practice. Making work that is socio-politically relevant, making performance that plays with the relationship between performer and audience, and developing work with a team through an inclusive methodology.

I remember studying *The Island* by Athol Fugard, John Kani and Winston Nshona and being struck by its urgency, simplicity and playfulness. They had to break apartheid laws as well as conventions of theatrical production to make and perform the play. It was illegal for black and white men to work together in this way and relatively new for actors to co-author a show. This developed my interest in how I could make work about the issues that are significant in my world now, so that I could perform in something that I cared about.

In moving to London I have realised that the things that interest me are big, global systems, habits and ideas that are not necessarily specific to one place. I am interested in violence, how human beings engage in it on a large scale. I am interested in migration, how as a race we are used to moving and why that is now becoming problematic. I am interested in belonging, how we come to belong and why we want to. I am interested in memory, individual, collective and selective.

There are artists that I really admire who are grappling with how to deal with these ideas creatively. I think that Richard Mosse's "Infra", a collection of photographs of the Democratic Republic of Congo through an infra red lens, in which the lush green of the landscape and militia in camouflage uniforms are turned a deep pink, truly encapsulates the violence that controls the country by making it something arrestingly beautiful.

One of the things that has fascinated me for a long time is genocide, not one specific genocide, but the fact that humanity has repeatedly taken part in this horrific action. In 2012 I went to Cambodia, largely due to my interest in the Cambodian genocide in which an estimated one and a half to three million people were killed. When I returned, I knew I wanted to make *No Feedback* with a group of people who were similarly intrigued and repelled by the subject of genocide and all that it opens up about who we are as human beings.

The No Feedback team all have individual interests in being part of the project as well as skills that offer a richness. Apart from being performers and performance makers we are anthropologists, biologists, facilitators, writers, teachers, designers, puppeteers and dancers.

Part of my work was to find a way of including this wealth of interests and concerns within how we made the show. We had to work openly enough to make this a group vision but be focused enough to actually produce something. There is a lot of trust in our process, as when we started we did not know where we would end up. I have taken a lot from the work of Forced Entertainment and in particular Tim Etchell's book *Certain Fragments* as well as *Body, Space, Image* by Miranda Tufnell and Chris Crickmay. The way these artists and researchers unpack and explore the devising process provides a springboard for developing our own model for creating work. All members of the team have engaged with the project generously and from their own perspective, so much so that this is really not my project anymore, but rather the formation of a performance company. It is incredible to be part of a process where we are all grappling with the difficulty of what we have taken on and trying to find a successful way of working together.

Finding the document *The Ten Stages of Genocide* and using it as an anchor for our research and development was an important methodological choice. This document is written by Gregory Stanton from Genocide Watch and is a working document for global genocide prevention. It has become the 'spine' of the show, the thing that holds it together. We have been privileged to have Greg's support for *No Feedback* and the constant reminder of the gravity of the subject we are dealing with.

What *The Ten Stages of Genocide* does so well is to argue that genocide is a process, starting from classifying one group of people as different to others, working through persecution and the mass killings that we commonly consider to be genocide, and ending with denial of these atrocities. The Armenian genocide and Turkey's lack of recognition of it have been spoken about a lot recently due to its 100 year anniversary. The framework of The Ten Stages allows this denial to be viewed as part of the genocide itself, rather than something after the fact. This seems like an important perspective and one that is key to genocide prevention in the future.

If I leave these conceptual and methodological concerns aside for a moment, what really drives me to perform is the space between me and the audience, the space where a connection can be made, the shared time and space that makes performance different from all other art forms. This idea is brilliantly captured by Marina Abramovic's *The Artist is Present,* in which that is all there is, the space between the artist and the single audience member who simply sit across a table from each other.

I want to take from this mode of 'performance art' and make the connection between the performer and the audience the most important element of the show.

This is the driving principal behind the immersive form of *No Feedback*. Can an artwork sit somewhere between Abramovic and the truly immersive worlds of Punchdrunk's shows? That is what I am trying to find out.

My work to date has played with the performer-audience connection in various ways by giving the audience different amounts of agency. *No Feedback* continues this exploration by making the audience's role essential to the completion of the piece. Inherent in this show is the risk of trusting the audience to make the show with us, and of asking them to engage with the difficult themes and ideas that it brings up. We want people to have fun and laugh and play with us and then leave thinking and talking about what it has triggered for them.

I trust that this is the beginning of a life for the show that will take many different forms and functions, being experienced across schools, community groups, museums, as well as arts venues, allowing us to demonstrate that this conversation involves all of us, from the playground to wherever our evolution takes us.

First published on littleatoms.com on 14 May 2015 as *The Anatomy of Mass Murder*

Occurrences of Genocide (this list is not exhaustive)

Vietnam	1471
Guatemala	1524 - 1983 multiple
Bolivia & Ecuador	1533 - 1550s
United States of America	1539 - 1890
Canada	1636 - 1870 multiple
Siberia	1640s - 1750s
Qing Dynasty/China	1755 - 1757
Peru	1780 - 1782
France	1793 - 1796
Haiti	1804
Zulu Kingdon/South Africa, Zimbabwe	1810 - 1828
Australia and Tasmania	1824 - 1908
Newfoundland	1829
New Zealand	1830s
Ireland	1845 - 1852
Mexico	1847 - 1901
Russian Empire	1860s
Japan	1869
Argentina	1870s, 1976 - 1983
Congo	1890 - 1908, 1996 - 2008
Namibia	1904 - 1907
Ottoman Empire/Turkey	1915 - 1938 multiple
Soviet Union	1919 - 1948 multiple
Kazakhstan	1926 - 1937
Tibet	1930s, 1950s - 1960s
Poland	1939 - 1948
Germany, Croatia, Yugoslavia	1941 - 1945
India	1947 - 1948, 1984, 2002
East Pakistan/Bangladesh	1971 - 1972
Burundi	1972, 1988, 1991, 1993
Chile	1973 - 1990
East Timor	1975 - 1999
Cambodia	1975 - 1979
Iraq	1982, 2005 - 2007
Kurdish region of Iraq	1987 - 1988
Brazil	1988
Sierra Leone	1991 - 2002
Rwanda	1994
Bosnia & Herzegovina	1995
North Korea	mid 1990s - present
Kosovo	1998 - 1999
Darfur region of Sudan	2003 - present

Data from: A, Jones. (2011) Genocide: A Comprehensive Introduction. Oxon: Routlegde

Theatre Delicatessen May 2015

Theatre Delicatessen

Jessica Brewster

Theatre Delicatessen exists to support the development of artists and their work, with a specific focus on innovative, boundary-breaking experiential work. Using a pioneering approach to building resources for artists by working with a range of businesses, it creates incredible spaces to work and play in, professional development opportunities, training and support, and project delivery.

Its core ambition is to support artists to sustain long-term innovative artistic careers that make a meaningful contribution to everyone who participates.

Our work with artists is in response to a rapidly changing British Theatre landscape. In responding to and reflecting on the huge techological and social changes occuring in our world, the theatrical form has grown way beyond the confines of traditional theatre space.

Theatre Delicatessen's focus is to support artists taking part in this incredible exploration of form and structure: interactivity, audience-led, site-specific/responsive, and immersive are just a few forms entering the mainstream of what had previously been trapped behind the "4th wall."

For us this diversity of form has created, alongside new technologies, a remarkable new set of tools for artists to explore the subjects, themes and issues that excite and engage them.

No Feedback was an obvious choice for support: using the mechanics of gaming and audience participation alongside rigorous physical performance to create a brand new, highly accessible piece about a difficult political subject.

Since our first encounter with them, at a scratch night in an old warehouse, they have not only developed an original artistic voice through the piece, but have become an increasingly strong company of collaborating artists.

But most excitingly for us at Theatre Delicatessen has been to watch how they have developed their artform to reach out to new audiences and new communities, using art to start important conversations about who we are, and how we think.

Anne Frank Trust

To challenge prejudice and reduce hatred by drawing on the power of Anne Frank's life and diary. To use that power to encourage people to embrace positive attitudes, personal responsibility, and respect for others.

@AnneFrankTrust   http://www.annefrank.org.uk/who-we-are/our-mission

We had significant discussions with members of the Anne Frank team about how audiences may respond to how we have dealt with this difficult subject matter and how the show may be taken into schools at a later date.

Centre for Postcolonial Studies at Goldsmiths, University of London

As postcolonial studies expanded beyond its origins in literary studies to an engagement with epistemological, ethical, aesthetic and political questions, this interdisciplinary Centre was created and housed in the Politics Department at Goldsmiths.

@pococentre   http://www.gold.ac.uk/postcolonial-studies/

The Centre provided us with support at the very beginning, when no one else would. This gave us the possibility to initiate our ideas and form a solid foundation for our work within a space of critical discourse. We continue to work with them on the future of the project.

Wiener Library

The Wiener Library is one of the world's leading and most extensive archives on the Holocaust and Nazi era. Formed in 1933, the Library's unique collection of over one million items includes published and unpublished works, press cuttings, photographs and eyewitness testimony.

@wienerlibrary   http://www.wienerlibrary.co.uk

The Wiener Library supported us immensely in the development of the show, providing invaluable and unique resources that directly shaped the production.

Genocide Watch

Genocide Watch exists to predict, prevent, stop, and punish genocide and other forms of mass murder. We seek to raise awareness and influence public policy concerning potential and actual genocide. Our purpose is to build an international movement to prevent and stop genocide.

@genocide_watch   http://genocidewatch.net

'The 10 Stages of Genocide' by Genocide Watch provided the root text for the development of the show. Once we found this document we started building an immersive performance around the idea of taking an audience through the stages.

People's Palace Projects

People's Palace Projects (PPP) is an independent arts charity that advances the practice and understanding of art for social justice. It is a National Portfolio organisation (NPO) of Arts Council England and is based at Queen Mary, University of London.

http://www.peoplespalaceprojects.org.uk/about/ @PeoplesPalaceUK

We have recently formed a partnership with People's Palace Projects to develop and roll out the next phase of No Feedback with Women's Rights International.

Remembering Srebrenica

Remembering Srebrenica is a British charitable initiative. It recognises that we have achieved a lot in terms of building a cohesive society here in the UK, but discrimination, promotion of hatred, extremism, and exclusion persist, and we must play our part, no matter how large or small, to create a better and safer society for all.

http://www.srebrenica.org.uk @SrebrenicaUK

We have been partnering with Remembering Srebrenica to highlight the fact that Genocides continue to happen all over the world. We are working with them to develop a version of No Feedback to be taken to the communities and schools that they work with.

Theatre Delicatessen

Theatre Delicatessen exists to support emerging artists, creatives and theatremakers in their work and the development of their practice.

http://theatredelicatessen.co.uk @theatredeli

Theatre Delicatessen is our home. They have allowed No Feedback to get to where it is today by hosting rehearsals and performances, providing artistic mentorship as well as production and marketing support.

Westminster Law and Theory Lab

The Westminster Law & Theory Lab brings together diverse yet overlapping strands in the study of law and theory, with a strong emphasis on interdisciplinarity, critical and sociolegal theoretical analysis.

http://www.westminster.ac.uk/law-and-theory/home @WLTcentre

Professor Andreas Philippopoulos-Mihalopoulos' discussions with us on the impact of legal theory on how prejudice operates in society were essential to helping us understand how to incorporate this area of concern into our performance.

67

Nina Feldman. Founding Artist/Ensemble.

Nina is a multidisciplinary artist who studied physical theatre and design at the University of the Witwatersrand in Johannesburg and Performance Making at Goldsmiths College, London. She is founding member of No Feedback and co-director of involuntarymovement, which works through dance and drama with people of varying abilities to create learning situations for social and creative development. Her work focuses on socio-political issues, global systems and performance practices.

Debora Minà. Founding Artist/Ensemble.

Debora is an Italian theatre maker and facilitator. Influenced by a background in Anthropology, her work is concerned with intercultural dialogue, belonging and how the creative process can contribute to the expansion of identity. She works in London and internationally in theatre for social change for Pan Intercultural Arts and she is a visiting tutor at Royal Central School of Speech and Drama and Goldsmiths College.

Genevieve Maxwell. Artist/Ensemble.

Genevieve is a performer, movement specialist and director with a background in Contemporary Dance Theatre, Somatics, Neuroscience and a degree in Anthropology. Her practice is transdisciplinary in nature, allowing for a dialogue between concept and form. In addition she is a longstanding collaborator and performer with Lundahl & Seitl, with whom she tours internationally, and has experience of leading workshops in particular with severely traumatised young people.

Carolin Ott. Artist/Ensemble.

Carolin is a bilingual German performer, deviser and theatre maker and is Lecoq and classically trained. She is a strong believer that theatre is and can be for everyone, and is interested in using different mediums to create stories and ask questions.

Jen Plants. Artist/Ensemble.

The Carl Djerassi Playwriting Fellow at the University of Wisconsin-Madison, Jen is an American actor, deviser and director whose work has appeared on stages from New York City to London. She earned her MFA at the Florida State University/Asolo Conservatory for Actor Training, founded the theatre program at Hood College in Frederick, Maryland, and focuses her current work on the collaborative process and the ways we performing othering on English-speaking stages.

Lizzie Sells. Artist/Ensemble.

A dancer by training, Lizzie works as a performer, choreographer and co-creator in cultural projects ranging from dance, theatre and opera to film, visual and live art. Running parallel to her performance practice, she works as a movement educator teaching creative dance and yoga to children and adults as well as movement coaching actors, singers and musicians.

Irène Wernli. Artist/Ensemble.

Irène is a collaborative performance deviser working across the genres of dance and theatre. She teaches movement across London, guest lectures at New Bucks University, and is currently studying Creative Producing for Live Performance and Theatre at Birkbeck University, London.

Andy Franzkowiak. Creative Producer.

An award winning creative producer, Andy specialises in science & art projects and site-specific theatre. His work includes the critically acclaimed Enlightenment Café (Deadinburgh, New Atlantis) - a series of multidisciplinary art and science collaborations; Utopia 2016, Somerset House; Minds Eye, an audio tour of the solar system by Shrinking Space; and projects with Punchdrunk, The Old Vic Tunnels, Southbank Centre, and BBC.

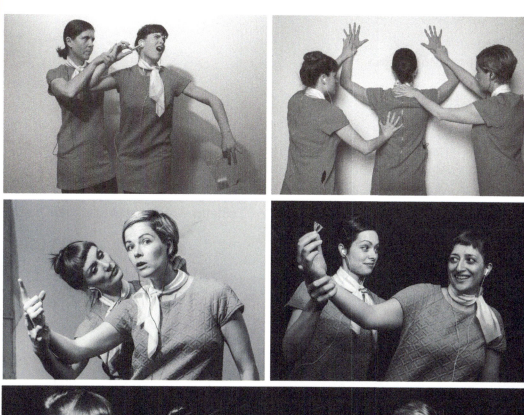

Credits

Photography

Andy Franzkoviak

4, 20, 26, 34, 35, 38, 39, 43, 44, 45, 51, 56, 57, 62, 63, back cover

Shana Swiss

6, 7, 8, 9

Will Jennings

front cover, 12,13, 21, 29, 50, 65

Lizzie Sells

27

Marco Monterzino

38, 39

Genevieve Maxwell

38

By Agriculture And Stock Department, Publicity Branch [Public domain], via Wikimedia Commons

43

By Archives New Zealand from New Zealand - Air Hostess Uniform 1959 Winter 005, CC BY-SA 2.0

44

By Archives New Zealand from New Zealand - Air Hostess Uniform 1970 Lollipop 001, CC BY-SA 2.0

44

Nina Feldman

3, 67

Book Design

Nina Feldman with Lizzie Sells

Lightning Source UK Ltd.
Milton Keynes UK
UKOW07f1317030616

275548UK00015B/85/P